No Sound But The Soul

Natasha Kronenberg

Presentation by *BookLeaf Publishing*

Web: www.bookleafpub.com

E-mail: info@bookleafpub.com

ISBN: 9789357614047

First edition 2022

dedicated to those robbed of an education
who will never read this book

ACKNOWLEDGEMENT

I would firstly like to acknowledge and thank the traditional custodians of the lands on which this poetry was written and inspired by, the Turrbal and Jagera people of the Brisbane region. The poetry, stories, art and culture of these Indigenous peoples were and continue to be silenced and oppressed by colonial powers causing generational trauma and disconnect. I feel so lucky and privileged to be creating on their traditional soils and strive to never forget its history. Sovereignty was never seeded, and inequality remains prevalent but may we strive for harmony, community and understanding between all Australians.

I would also like to thank Nikita (ink.eyta) for her wonderful friendship and belief in me as a writer. She is such a beautiful soul and I owe much of my poetic self to her.

Finally, I'd like to thank my wonderful parents and friends for surrounding me in positive environments and fostering my love for the arts. Words cannot describe the gratitude I feel for my parents' prioritisation of life experience and artistic exploration over material possession. I also wish to thank Madison, my best friend who has always been a calming and supportive voice in my life. Her honesty, love, reliability, and kindness has been the sunshine to my many storms.

PREFACE

Much like falling in love with a person, I can never pick the exact day or time when poetry inched its way into my heart.

Born in 2003, most people wouldn't expect my childhood to be as analogue as it was, but my mother's love of literature and attentive parenting meant my nights were spent curled up listening to her read Dr. Seuss, the Narnia chronicles, Hairy McClary and of course Harry Potter. Though I never truly realised it, I grew up in an extremely artistic household. My father was an actor, puppeteer and acrobat by trade and my mother had been involved with circus for most of her life. As a family, even after my parents' separation we would all go to the theatre, music events or circus shows together. This inspired me to dance, sing and perform from a young age despite toxicity in many of the creative environments I grew up in.

My love affair with literature grew further in high school where I distinctly remember tears welling in my eyes listening to both T.S Eliot and William Butler Yeats for the first time. The way these authors, particularly Eliot, gave words to feelings I hadn't been able to express was both astounding and jarring to me.

I graduated school busting to expand my horizons and leave my town of Albury in NSW. I packed up and moved to Brisbane alone, itching for the sunshine and new possibilities. I soon became engulfed in the artistic community and eventually became involved with dance, poetry, acting and circus companies.

Now as a fledgling adult I'm slowly sprouting my artistic wings and discovering what sort of impact I want to have on the world. Along this journey I've continuously written poetry and prose some of which you will read in this anthology. I hope you enjoy this collection and thank you so much for taking the time to see the world through my eyes.

A Brisbane Love Story

It was 5am in Meanjin, Autumn, still dark
The city day was yet to begin
and all was silent in Musgrave Park

The early-morning tradies drove down the
empty streets
And it was here in West End
Where our two wheeled companions would meet

Neurons platform was sturdy, had driven many
people home
Yet his lopsided handlebars drooped
Noticing he was all alone

It had been a tough night, full of gutters and
squashed cans
He sat there, broken, and exhausted
Just waiting for the battery man

It was at this moment, when the dawn lit the
skies
That Neuron's depression was disrupted
Much to the scooter's surprise

A lone drunk, clumsy and smelling of Gin

Scooted up on two wheels
Parking his Beam scooter right beside him

The man hiccupped stumbling away into the
dark
Neurons lights looked up
For now there were two in Musgrave Park

Neuron stole a quick glance then stared at the
ground
He was self-conscious of his scratched-up
surface
To which his purple companion frowned

It was true, she thought, Neuron had seen better
days
But the signs of his hard work were charming
So she held the orange scooter's gaze

"I'm Beam," she started, with stars in her lights.
"You've definitely brightened my morning
already,"
"May I stay?" she said to his delight.

"Not at all I'm rather glad you're here,
These lonesome nights are a bore
Well, that was, until you appeared."

Though competitors in the urban transport
market, they shared the same blood
Afterall red was in purple and orange
Thus neuron thought…..was it possible for love?

They were back and forth with chatter all
morning long
Talking of funny stories
And simply getting along

All of a sudden, around noon Beam's head
began to bow
Neuron panicked, "What's the matter?"
"I think my charge is out, at least for now."

"No No" he cried, "Please don't leave me yet,"
"Don't worry, Neuron," she said.
"Yours is a face I would never forget."

"We'll see each other soon then?" He shakily
asked
"Of course we will," Gleamed the scooter
"This encounter is far from our last."

It was with these final words that Beams lights
blinked out
Neuron sighed yet he was happy
For now he had a friend, without a shadow of a
doubt.

Tree Trauma

Wooden floorboards know not of the winters which ailed their arboreous ancestors. Those Grandma eucalypts which inhaled our sickness, endured our winters of hostility and housed our forgotten friends with no debt to be repaid. She is a symbol of ultimate sacrifice, ringed with age and stretched out with wisdom. Unaffected yet all-knowing of the goings on in the world, the smog which slowly seeps into her leaves and the slow decrease of her friends. A testament to the old times she stands, housing the memories of the past in her gum nuts, sewn by the winds of the before.

The winds of the now bring her new challenges, and eventually a departure from the soils. These soils, this country. On which she has existed; before country meant rivalry. All of her existence, ceased by a steely axe sinking into the sap. Tears of the galaxy spill like syrup from their contained infinity with arachnids and insects alike frozen in their pain for eternity. An amber universe. Eventually we make use of this cosmos. Give her functionality, and an irrelevant monetary value. We adorn ourselves with these dimensions and construct our own worlds with the bones of the tree, devoid of history. I know not of the winters which ailed my family tree, but you may see when those ambers finally spill from me.

The Box

I always knew there was a box
I always knew it would be locked.
You keep it safe under your bed
You keep it safe beneath our heads.

Before we ever meet
Before we ever lay
You take your heart
And you lock it away.

You and I we are not sleeping
You and I we are not dreaming
I borrow your flesh
I borrow your soul

But it's your fragile heart
That my coarse hands shall never hold.

Injustice

The injustice in my heart unfurls her lanky
hands, gripping onto the last morsel of my sanity
which rocks and sways in the seas of despair.
She becomes the ocean, a tidal wave of betrayal
which drowns
Out all ration. I feel her waters replace my
blood, gushing through the veins of my mind
then pooling in my eyes.
Before her shores can reach the beaches of
politeness, they come gushing out my mouth and
I scream.

Winston's Date

Winston sat awkwardly, a nervous ball of
anticipation. He chose the corner table of the
restaurant furthest from the door.
Furthest from his flaws, the uncomfortable
pauses and of course all the causes of his
previous divorce.
Another sip of water, a glance at his watch.
He watched the flocks of frocks and curly locks
mock him

Him and his loneliness clawing onto the breath
of life in the shape of a lover
To give his love to another
He hoped.

And just as the knots in his fingers could not
squeeze his soul any tighter he looked and
lingered.
There she stood, glancing the room giving every
inch of the atmosphere the pleasure of her gaze

There was a message in those eyes and to
Winston's surprise he heard the cries of
Someone just like him.
He saw the child within

Deprived of the gift he was so willing to give

Despite her beauty the world insisted on
spinning as he kept grinning at the thought of
their beginning
She floated towards him with elegance and style
framed by her smile
Of perfect white teeth
Winston cleared his throat, "Take a seat," he said
With a nod of his head

The angel stood for a moment then floated from
her cloud to meet him across the table
From that moment forth there was non-stop
chatter, about this matter and that matter
And his attempts to flatter

In her heart she knew that their love would
renew
All the dead forests of broken promises
She wanted to grow old with him, watch his hair
gray and body decay
As she stood by his side

He was entranced by her curling song of
affection
The perfect lips which curled and dipped in
phrases of worship

Their conversation carried on without a fight, far
past midnight
Until the moon shone above
Brilliant and bright

Care for tea? He asked politely, to which she did
agree
Perfect teeth beaming with glee.

Winston's apartment was small, unassuming but
she loved that in him
The charm which accompanied a gentleman
with only the most basic furnishing
Soon, just as the wallpaper peeled from the wall
So did her clothes which softly hit the floor
He grazed her arm with his fingers, paused a
moment to linger

Before snapping her neck with a swift crack
Slowly her eyes rolled back
and her entire consciousness went black

Crossing the floor he reached into the draw,
retrieving a pair of sturdy pliers
Unfortunately, she was a necessary victim
He couldn't let perfect teeth simply tempt him

Kneeling to the floor he straddled her jaw and
slowly plucked them

One by one
He studied his handy-work with a contented sigh
for he knew her price would be high

From across the world flocked the wealthy elite
Nothing on the homewares market was finer
He made his way through deception and deceit
Grinding molars into the most exquisite China.

Noise

Considering those existences for which are pointless without the curious eyeballs of examination to live under the rule of aristotle's pencil. Which glasshouse shall your butterings of toast and brushings of teeth be observed I ask you? It is to be established beyond all reasonable doubt that the upward trajectory of the somewhat puzzling instances of forgetting the security of one's transportation vehicle on the wonderings if and when in the pitiful cycles of shoe laces being tied and stamps being licked will you wait or hop to the bus. Go card? For whomst who has paid their fare share of transportation with the colonisation of THEIR lands. Oh yes do that! It'll help justify your purpose! Demand those payments in and out of the pockets of the 99 into the 1 so they all keep churning like the butter on the wheels. Peel the eyes like the oranges which grow from your arms, twigs in the hay house to be blown in and out by the wolf of doubt. You say you handle the storms, but they slap you with their thunder and the rain falls upwards like the bubbles in the rubber dub tub. We tub ourselves in the streets on around and through the gutters on the 6th day

of God's week when we bubble our blood until it
feels finally bearable to return forwards upward
into the hill that has become our week. A weak
week characterised by the characters we never
wrote into our stories who insist on the stapler
being filled and the notes being scrawled upon
while they sprawled upon their ticking and
clicking and sending and stamping and stomping
through their rhythms of occupations. Ties tied
to the taught tires which screech the earth and
bleach the reef and this person did these things
to those people and that person should've known
better. Well avocados are making their way onto
the tacos of the students yet these tacos still
reside in shacks which cost more than they
should. Why would I, how should I? You have
many ideas I'm sure of the writings of the future
but you never wrote the prologue did you? Ahhh
yes we forgot that, isn't it funny how prologues
are pro fog, pro backlog, pro smog and pro
podge. I wish to log my own pro in the fog yet in
doing so unclog the drains which drain me in the
training of straining. Why should I be braining
when I can be complaining? You'd ask me to
explain? Well haven't thy been receiving my
pleadings of pleasings and easings? The air
wobbles you know, frightfully so until we all go
where those old ones go.

Then and only then can we breathe.

Toothpaste

My toothpaste watches me every morning from
her perch on my enamel sink.
I've come to measure my life in tubes of
toothpaste.

She looks at me sadly, as if knowing that one
day I'll squeeze her dry then cut her open,
salvaging the entrails.

Night and day, the poor thing gets to witness my
furious,
Futile attempts
to cleanse my mouth of its bitter taste

The taste left by the 'polite whistle' which my
brain shoves
between my lips in the place of authenticity.

The bitter tang of the words
"Sorry, it's complicated but thanks so much for
the ride
I'll see you next week."

Rather than

"Please don't touch me again, I've told you that's not okay."

If I keep this up, I'll probably get a cavity.

I Only Have Eyes for Robert Timms

I only have eyes for one man, you may have
heard of him
He sits in the coffee aisle, quiet and unassuming
His name is Robert Timm

His love is the easy sort, a low pressure kinda
guy
He's always there when I need him
And requires no percolator to satisfy

It's his simple love I crave when I awake in the
morning
Just a bland cup of Joe with milk
Is all I need to keep me going

Nespresso snobs upturn their noses when I speak
about my man
Cafe goers curse to the gods
And Starbucks princesses, they'd never
understand

The caffeinated masses, the ones willing to
spend every dime
On the perfect tall late

Think instant fixes are a crime

What these high strung citizens can never
understand
Is the value of a convenient love
Such is the worth of a Timms man

Whether you in the office or simply on the street
Away on a camping trip
Or still between the sheets

Roberts basic love is always dear and true
So leave the caramel behind
And get some good old Robert in you

A Sick Sixth Sense

I was taught much like you were of the inconveniences of our anatomy in the modern world. Our fast metabolism which can't keep up with the junk we ingest and cram into our brains. Our adrenaline which hooks us to hookers and bookers and poker machines and the in-betweens. Our hair which no longer can cleanse itself naturally from the smog and smoke so sends us broke buying chemicals to balance it out. It's true, I slave away to these physiological inconveniences too, yet I have another view.

I noticed this rather helpful present from the past when I met you. Could not HELP but notice it in fact. The twisting of my entrails when the twisting of pasta you paid for entered my stomach. Heavier than before, paid for by your……generosity, excuse my animosity but you see, my sixth sense could forsee. The causality of all transparency. The niceties which wiggled their way between our conversation. The way the venues we visited created a blacklist in my head, how the floor of those places seem to hold our footsteps even now. Our footsteps which were too close together yet too far for the sixth sense to pick up on. She had the flu that day, an induced sickness caused by politeness, ethanol and practices drilled into us. She was shackled by the cuffs of our mutual friends and fear of making things awkward. Tied down by the awful transition from no to maybe to argument to…..I suppose so.

I faced her the next morning when I looked in your mirror. She stared back at me with tense shoulders, frozen from a paralysed night and eyes which had been peeled open in the dark that now hung out like a drunk over a railing. The thing I saw the most was her disappointment, glaringly obvious in her smirk. The kind of 'I told you so' pill which I gulped down with a handful of water from the sink.

I'm nursing her now, after that ordeal. We're doing better, my sixth sense and I. I take her with me in my guarded stare and challenging glare. I'm trying to make amends so one day we shall be friends, my sick sixth sense and I.

Inconveniences

Despite those inconveniences
Which lead one's mind astray
Like over filling a coffee cup
Or when the trains delay

When dog shit's left on the footpath
Or keys left in the door
When seeds are stuck between your teeth
Or work just seems a bore

Loud planes, food stains
Clogged drains, back pains
Which seem to render life mundane

Still are insignificant to the joys
Through which we are sustained

Poem for the Shining One

I did not realise that my life would change.
Could not foresee or fore-hear the words which
would change me. I suppose that's the ongoing
joke life makes about you, the source of its
smirk. How it so diligently places figurines in
the exact location and waits……for chaos or
beauty I'm not sure. Well life decided on that
evening purposefully or not, to surround me
with books, couches, a microphone and you. I
remember the night like it was tomorrow.

You held your fragility by its throat, in your
shaking delicate hands. Stared it down before
you, whispering, I am more than that man.
Streams of wonder pooled in my eyes and to my
shock and surprise you took these cries and
coiled them into ropes of wire. So strong you
could suspend bridges from it. I clung to this
taught pain, and swung from it, letting go and
diving into your linguistic universe face first.

 The golden oceans of your ideas filled my lungs
with syrup and I could breathe. The scent of
your story smelt like burnt caramel popcorn. So
sweet yet tinged with the fire of pain. These

golden rivers didn't stop. I didn't know to pack
my bathing suit, wasn't dressed for the weather
one could say because these sentences drenched
my soul until it touched my bones. I don't wish
to dry off.

These golden waves lapped at my conscience for
only 7 minutes before I was hatched out of this
universe and back into the basement. I stilled
myself from the vertigo and watched you retreat
from the platform. Watched you mask on and
become what's expected of you but we had all
seen. There was no un-wittnessing you.

Departure

Keys left in doors long aged and cobwebbed

Crystal glasses with little more than memories of
previous poisons

Skeletal spiders embracing themselves in final
comfort

Weeping candles lusting for flame once more

Still, I peeled back the umbrella and kissed you
amidst the torrent of the storm
denying the inevitability of our epilogue

A silent coda strummed from the torn strings of
a double bass

The weariness of existence lulled its head

Exhaling, all that ever was collapsed

And the ceiling knelt in the holiness of its
wreckage

Bushfire Sleigh Ride

I hear that fire truck ring a ring
Ding ding, ding-a-ling too
Hurry up, it's deadly weather
To be outside together with you

The sky is thick with smoke
And the kids are asking why
Just turn on the telly and
Watch more government lies

The children are crying
While the wildlife is dying too
Over'a million hectares
And it's not even through
There's no more water at the home of Farmer
Gray
It all went to coal and now it's flushed away

Tango

We both know this dance
Of its steps we are fully aware
Arms poised; chests lifted
Captured in the other's stare

The Tango of our conversation
A glance, a smile
A touch if one can risk it
Only to be followed by quick denial

So dance with me, my love
Restrain your kiss of affection
Keep that longing behind your eyes
Till one dares ask the question

Airport Boredom Poems

For this performance
I present a short haiku
Sadly that was it

I want some more kale
Far too much ice cream I've had
Said no one ever

I misplaced my keys
Grotesque mess inside my room
Must clean to find them

Wife beater singlet
Yells at cyclists on roads
I'll avoid that one

Stories

Give me your stories so that I may carry them
with my bones
Inside my bones, where the history of the stars is
created with the marrow.
For if not story, what am I? The chip in my
tooth, the dent in my head or the swelling of my
heart at the memory of you, I am story through
and through

Did those fish know, millenia ago, that the
mirrors of their scales would one day grow
feathers and tails? Or the horse which gallops
the song of the wind, mane forged in the earth's
early flame.

On the city streets and in the busy corridors of
occupation where the smoke of amnesia and
pretence pollute the music of the story, we are
blind to our history.

The old ones knew this, they did. Walked slowly
between the cracks and hills of time with their
bare feet, listening to country. The sorrow, the
laughter in the soles of their feet. The soles, the
soles, why call it this you may ask. For in the

footprints, we have soul, marking the beaches
with our stories.

So do me the great honour my love. Worship my
ears with the grace of your phrase and give to
me that which will outlast my final days.

What happened to you?

I can only just recall you on your first day of
school
Mum knew
Despite spending money on your scuffy shoes
That you'd grow out of them too soon
No longer her bubba-boo

Though sad, your mother was not bitter
For she knew your mind would grow quicker
The years would pass
From class to class
Pens and paper
Would become your nature

You held your innocence by the hand
With no way to understand
The ability for one to be mean
Or threaten, or tease or scream

It was a true shame
That there was an undetected game
Which your pure mind could not comprehend
And your sweet nature could not fend

The chess game of the playground

In which the meanest were crowned
The monarchs of the pack
To whom no one dared talked back

In these cages your soul retreated
As you were mistreated
Till your drunken naivety
Became cold sobriety

You once plaited hair
Now framed a steely stare
Never what you were before
Guarded and broken forevermore

A Letter to Busyness

Dear Busyness,

I think we need to review our relationship. It's not that I don't appreciate you, sometimes the fear of being stagnant is what gets me up and out of bed. But sadly, I think our relationship is one-sided. You see, you seem to take over sometimes. You're clingy, hogging all my free time and peace of mind.

Maybe you need a holiday, we all do. Courtesy of the house, as host of this establishment, I wish to grant you a holiday and casual position. We all need a break and with this new arrangement I think we will become closer and finally understand each other. Once you were a lifeline, kept me moving and protected me as a child from the frightening stillness but things have changed.

I now wish to bathe in that stillness alone, in the dark without the static of occupation. Soaking in the waters of realisation so that I may become more whole. Not because I'm doing more but because I'm okay with doing less. Doing less is

not less, those moments between breaths give
life.

So thank you, but I've changed and I won't rely
on you anymore for the reassurance that my
place in the world is not wasted.

With love,
The Host

Salsa Memorial

Enjoyed dancing with him I never much did
Yet when a wrinkled hand extended in plea I
wouldn't dare resist
Creased silk shirt desperately seeking warmth
from an emaciated frame beneath
And finding no comfort.
Sunken eyes above quivering lips which looked
at me with harrowing kindness.
I hold his sorrowful hand and shuffle with him
between the corridors of his ghosts

He carves epitaphs with his shoes telling all
which cannot be said
A wife, a home, a family long gone and long
dead
We dance among the tombstones and far into the
past
Clinging my heart to his, as though this salsa
were his last